Cave and Underground Homes

Debbie Gallagher

A⁺
Smart Apple Media

This edition first published in 2008 in the United States of America by Smart Apple Media.

Smart Apple Media
2140 Howard Drive West
North Mankato, Minnesota 56003

First published in 2007 by
MACMILLAN EDUCATION AUSTRALIA PTY LTD
627 Chapel Street, South Yarra, Australia 3141

Visit our Web site at www.macmillan.com.au or go directly to www.macmillanlibrary.com.au

Associated companies and representatives throughout the world.

Library of Congress Cataloging-in-Publication Data

Gallagher, Debbie, 1969-
    Cave and underground homes / by Debbie Gallagher.
    p. cm. — (Homes around the world)
    Includes index.
    ISBN 978-1-59920-155-9
    1. Cave architecture—Juvenile literature. 2. Earth sheltered houses—Juvenile literature. I. Title.

    NA8455.G35 200
    728.09144—dc22

                                                                2007004647

Edited by Angelique Campbell-Muir
Text and cover design by Christine Deering
Page layout by Domenic Lauricella
Photo research by Legend Images
Illustration by Domenic Lauricella

Printed in U.S.

Acknowledgements

The author and the publisher are grateful to the following for permission to reproduce copyright material:

Cover photograph: Cave home in Cappadocia, Turkey © Jonathan Blair/CORBIS/Australian Picture Library.

© john angerson/Alamy, pp. 25, 26; © Peter Bowater/Alamy, pp. 3, 21; © Rob Cousins/Alamy, p. 22; © Danita Delimont/Alamy, p. 14; © Denny Rowland/Alamy, p. 27; © Jonathan Blair/CORBIS/Australian Picture Library, pp. 1, 13, 15; © Stephanie Maze/CORBIS/Australian Picture Library, p. 18; © Breck/Dreamstime.com, p. 30 (center left); © Brownm39/Dreamstime.com, p. 30 (bottom right); © Wormold I Dreamstime.com, pp. 6 (centre), 12; © GOH CHAI HIN/AFP/Getty Images, p. 17; © iStockphoto.com/Eric Bechtold, p. 30 (top right); © iStockphoto.com/Jacques Croizer, pp. 5, 30 (top left); © iStockphoto.com/Angus Forbes, p. 7 (top), 20; © Lonely Planet Images/John Banagan, p. 11; © Lonely Planet Images/John Hay, pp. 6 (top), 8; © Mark Moxon, www.moxon.net, p. 30 (bottom left); © Michael Spencer/Saudi Aramco World/PADIA, p. 30 (center right); © Photolibrary/Index StockImagery, pp. 10, 23; © Photolibrary/Panorama Media (Beijing) Ltd., 6 (bottom), pp. 16, 19; © Photolibrary/Photononstop, p. 4; © Photolibrary/Robin Smith, p. 9; © Rick Ohanian, Undergroundhomes.com, pp. 7 (bottom), 24.

Contents

Glossary words

When a word is printed in **bold**, you can look up its meaning in the glossary on page 31.

Shelter

Everyone needs shelter, as well as food and water, warmth, and protection. Homes around the world provide shelter for people.

These are cave homes in France.

People live in many different types of homes.
Some people live in homes dug into hills and cliffs.
Some people live in homes underground.

This pit home in Africa is built underground.

Cave and underground homes

Some cave homes are dug into soft dirt hillsides. Others are natural caves that have formed in rocky cliffs.

At Coober Pedy, Australia, people have dug their homes into the desert sand.

In Turkey, some people live in cave homes made in chimney-shaped landforms.

Millions of families live in yaodong homes across the north of China.

Cave homes are often found in places where the weather is very hot. They provide good protection from the heat.

Many people in Andalusia, Spain, live in white cave homes.

Around the world thousands of families live in earth-sheltered homes.

Coober Pedy dugout

Coober Pedy, Australia, is very hot during the day and very cold at night. Most people there are miners digging for opal. They live in homes built underground.

Coober Pedy is a mining town built on a stony desert.

Dugouts are shelters dug into hillsides or underground. Some sections are widened into rooms. Dugouts are protected from the harsh temperatures outside.

openings for air and light

water tanks

slope

front entrance

Not much of a dugout is visible from above the ground.

Inside a Coober Pedy dugout

It can be quite dark inside a dugout. Many homes have extra **shafts** to the surface covered with glass, to let light in. Families can add rooms as needed.

electric lights

walls and ceiling left rough

Dugout homes also have electric lights.

Before people made dugout homes, it was very difficult to live at Coober Pedy. Homes above the ground now have air conditioning to keep them cool.

Today, Coober Pedy has homes above the ground and underground.

Cappadocian cave home

In Cappadocia, Turkey, there are thousands of tall rock cones. These were made by an ancient volcano and by **erosion**. Long ago people hollowed out the rock to make homes.

People call these rock cones "Fairy chimneys."

Cappadocian cave homes are **multileveled**. Storage rooms are at the lowest levels with family rooms above them. Cave openings let in fresh air.

The different levels are joined by stairs or ladders.

Inside a Cappadocian cave home

The walls inside the cave are painted white. In the main room, there is often a fireplace for cooking and heating.

electrical wires

painted walls

storage shelves on walls

Modern cave homes have electricity for cooking and lighting.

The cave homes stay cool and dark even on the hottest summer days. They are easily heated during very cold winters.

Cave openings let fresh air into the home.

Yaodong

For thousands of years, people in northern China have built yaodongs. Yaodongs are made by digging into the sides of steep hills.

The soil in this part of China is easy to dig.

Each yaodong has a wall built across the front called a **facade**. The facade has three **arched** doorways with windows to let air into the home.

facade

arched doorways with windows

The facade is made of stone or bricks found locally.

Inside a yaodong

The middle door leads to the living area inside a yaodong. Sleeping rooms are on each side. Cooking is done in the living area.

arched ceiling

inside walls covered with plaster

line for hanging clothes

storage cupboard

stovetop

In the living area, there is large stovetop used for cooking.

The weather in northern China can be very hot or very cold. The temperature underground stays comfortable. Yaodongs need little heating in winter and no cooling in summer.

Villages include yaodongs and non-cave buildings.

Andalusian cave home

There are more cave homes in Andalusia, Spain, than anywhere else in Europe. Cave homes stay cool in summer which is good because Andalusia can get very hot.

Terraces on cave homes are used for growing plants and drying foods.

Andalusian cave homes are built with a white facade across the front of the hillside. The facade has a small door and one or two windows.

Chimneys are tunneled through the top of the cave.

Inside an Andalusian cave home

Inside the cave home there are **alcoves** for storage. A fireplace is used for heating. The bathroom and kitchen are at the front of the home.

white walls

personal belongings hang on walls

furnishings

tiled floor

Walls and ceilings inside the cave are painted white.

The ceilings inside are high and round. Arched doorways separate the rooms. These curved shapes make the home stronger and keep them from **caving in**.

Tile floors have cement under them to keep the cave from getting damp.

Earth-sheltered house

An earth-sheltered house is made by digging a hole in the ground. The dirt removed is used to cover the finished house.

The roof and sides of an earth-sheltered house can be covered with grass or gardens.

The **foundation** of concrete or stone is put in the bottom of the hole. Concrete walls and a roof are added, then covered with dirt.

air vents

glass windows

roof and sides covered with dirt

door

outdoor area

One wall is left uncovered for doors and windows.

Inside an earth-sheltered house

Inside an earth-sheltered house there are separate rooms for sleeping, relaxing, and cooking. There are **skylights** in the roof and electric lights inside.

inside walls

large windows for light

floor

Windows let in plenty of natural light.

Earth-sheltered homes use less **energy** to keep them warm or cool. They are also safer than houses above the ground during storms.

Earth-sheltered homes blend into the area around them.

Floor plan

This is a **floor plan** of a Cappadocian cave home. It gives you a "bird's-eye view" of the rooms inside the home.

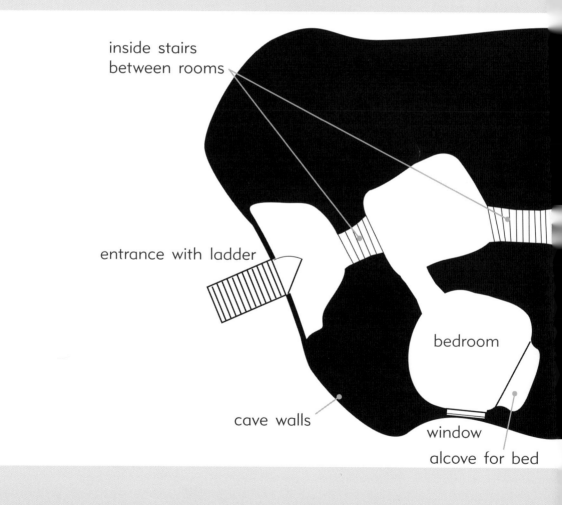

inside stairs between rooms

entrance with ladder

bedroom

cave walls

window

alcove for bed

Try this!

Draw a floor plan of your home. Label all the spaces, inside and outside, as well as features such as doors and windows.

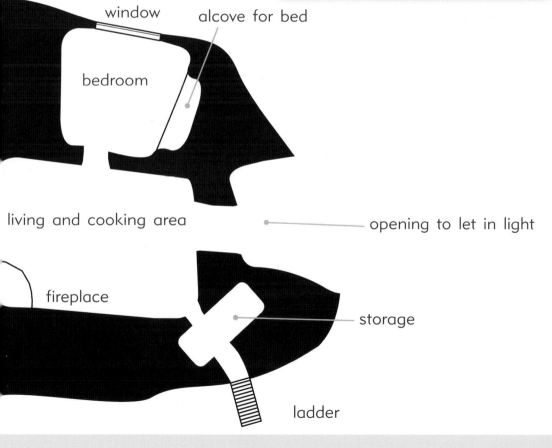

window

alcove for bed

bedroom

living and cooking area

opening to let in light

fireplace

storage

ladder

Homes around the world

There are many different types of homes around the world. All homes provide shelter for the people who live in them.

A pit home in Africa

New York City apartments

Windsor Castle in London

Mud and grass homes

Tuareg tent in the Sahara Desert

Lake home in Asia

Glossary

alcoves   small spaces that are set into a wall

arched   curved, like an upside-down U shape

caving in   collapsing

dugouts   homes made by digging into the ground or into the side of a slope, mostly used in mining or military situations

energy   power, such as gas or electricity

erosion   the wearing away of something by wind and water

facade   the front of a building

floor plan   a drawing that shows the layout of the areas in a home or building, as if seen from above

foundation   the base on which something sits

multileveled   having more than one level, or floor, in a house or building

shafts   narrow holes or passageways

skylights   flat windows in a roof used to let in light

Index